FINGER GUITAR STYLE
NOTES & TAB

CHILDREN'S SONGS

T0041088

ISBN 0-634-04299-8

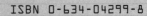

HAL•LEONARD® CORPORATION

7777 W. BLUEMOUND RD. P.O. BOX 13819 MILWAUKEE, WI 53213

Visit Hal Leonard Online at
www.halleonard.com

CONTENTS

Beauty and the Beast

from Walt Disney's BEAUTY AND THE BEAST

Lyrics by Howard Ashman
Music by Alan Menken

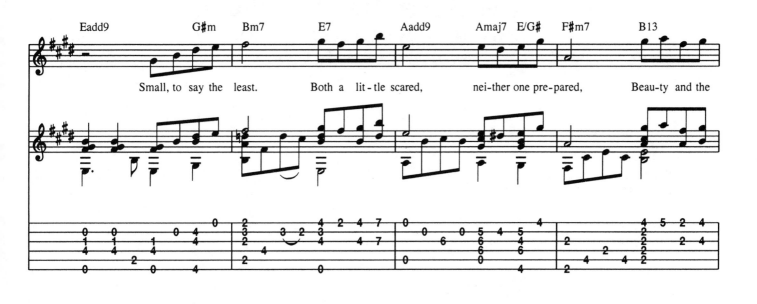

Small, to say the least. Both a lit-tle scared, nei-ther one pre-pared, Beau-ty and the

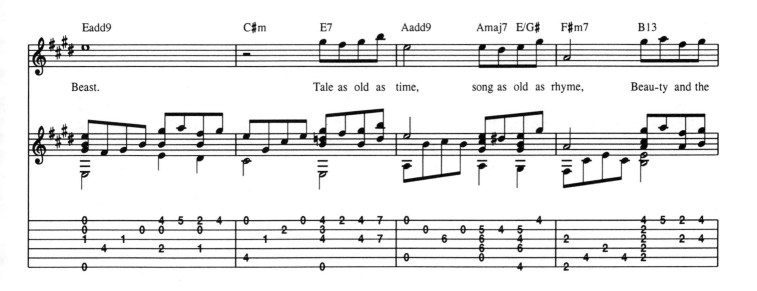

Beast. Tale as old as time, song as old as rhyme, Beau-ty and the

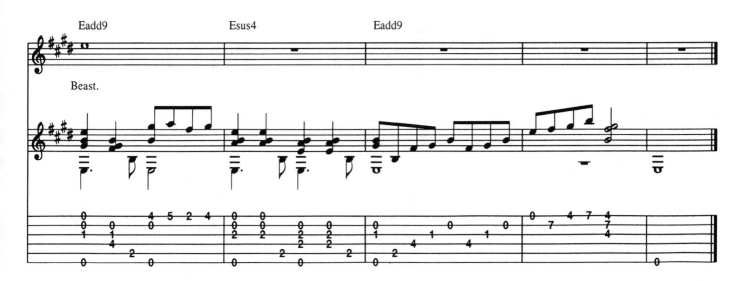

Beast.

The Bare Necessities

from Walt Disney's THE JUNGLE BOOK

Words and Music by Terry Gilkyson

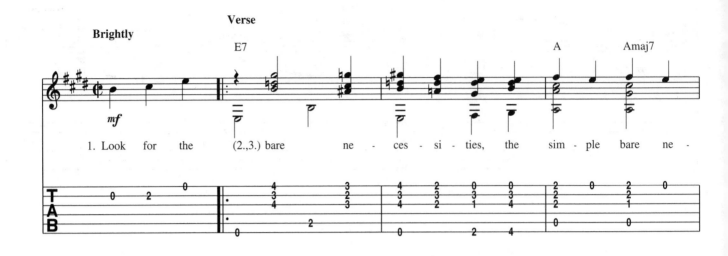

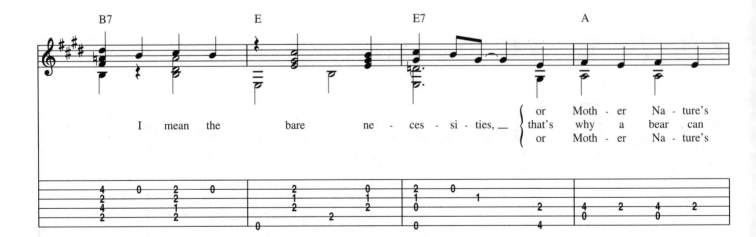

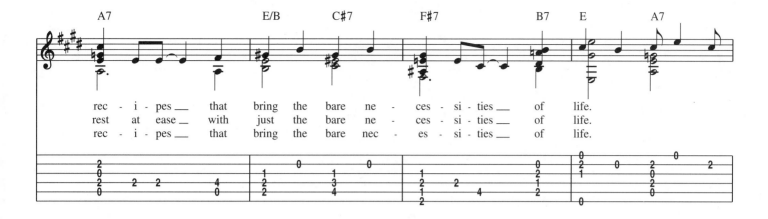

rec - i - pes __ that bring the bare ne - ces - si - ties __ of life.
rest at ease __ with just the bare ne - ces - si - ties __ of life.
rec - i - pes __ that bring the bare nec - es - si - ties __ of life.

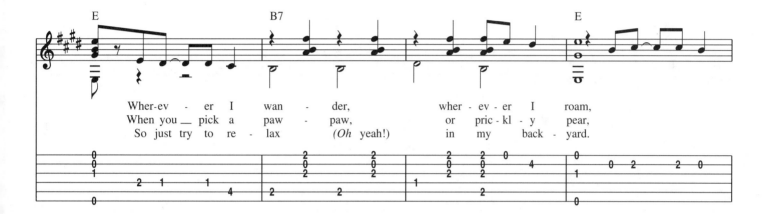

Wher-ev - er I wan - der, wher - ev - er I roam,
When you __ pick a paw - paw, or pric - kl - y pear,
So just try to re - lax (Oh yeah!) in my back - yard.

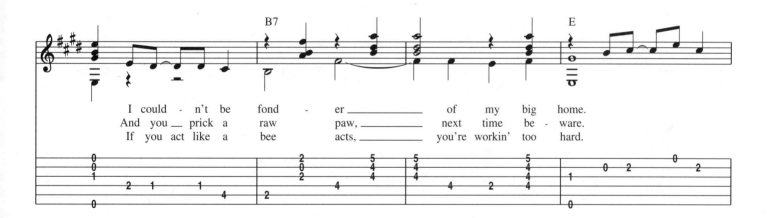

I could - n't be fond - er __ of my big home.
And you __ prick a raw paw, __ next time be - ware.
If you act like a bee acts, __ you're workin' too hard.

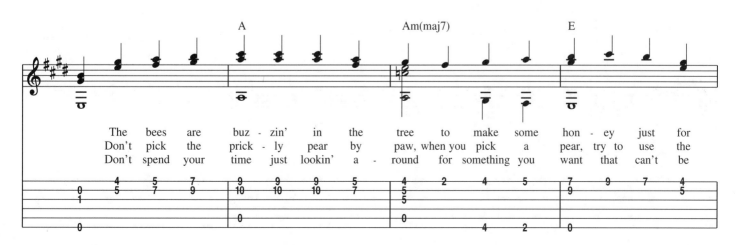

The bees are buz-zin' in the tree to make some hon - ey just for
Don't pick the prick - ly pear by paw, when you pick a pear, try to use the
Don't spend your time just lookin' a - round for something you want that can't be

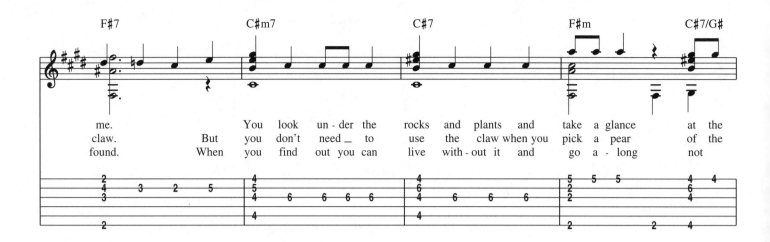

me.
claw.
found.

You look un-der the
But you don't need to
When you find out you can

rocks and plants and
use the claw when you
live with-out it and

take a glance at the
pick a pear of the
go a-long not

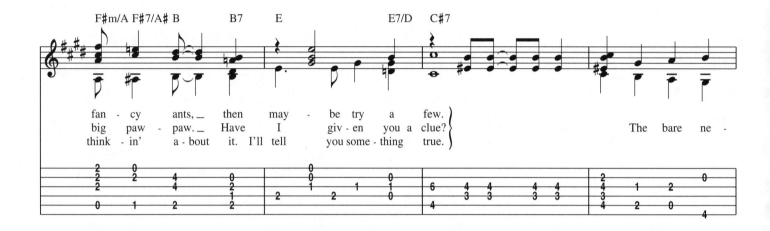

fan - cy
big paw - paw.
think - in'

ants, then may - be try a
Have I giv - en you a
a - bout it. I'll tell you some - thing

few.
clue?
true.

The bare ne -

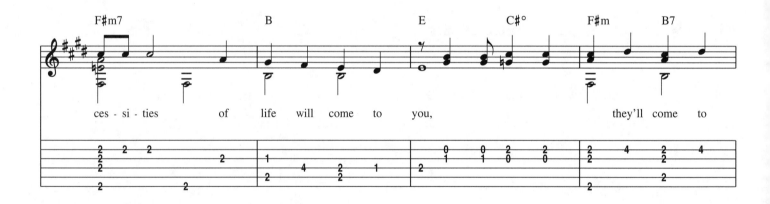

ces - si - ties of life will come to you, they'll come to

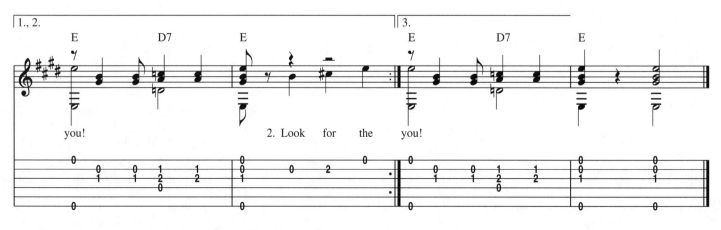

you! 2. Look for the you!

The Candy Man

from WILLY WONKA AND THE CHOCOLATE FACTORY

Words and Music by Leslie Bricusse and Anthony Newley

Verse
Brightly

1. Who can take a sun - rise, _____ sprin - kle it with dew, _____
2., 3. *See additional lyrics*

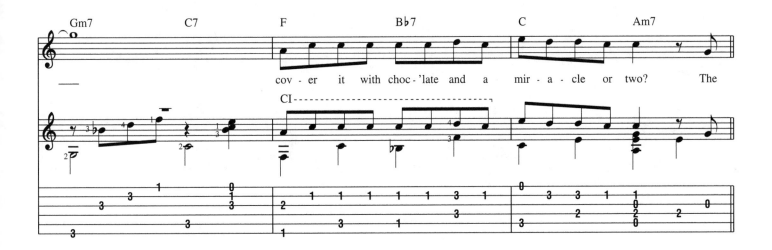

cov - er it with choc - 'late and a mir - a - cle or two? The

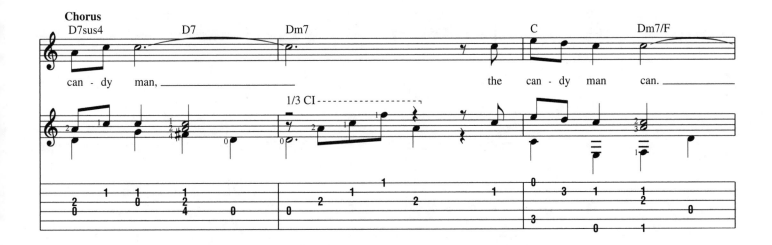

Chorus

can - dy man, _____ the can - dy man can. _____

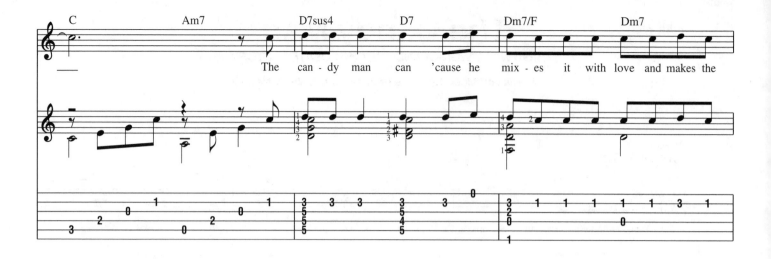

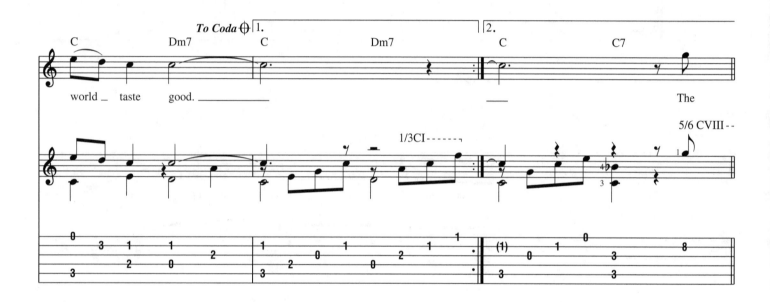

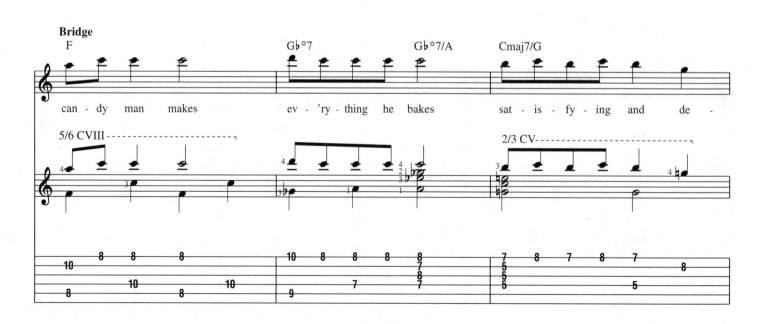

li - cious.　　　Talk a - bout your child - hood wish - es!

D.C. al Coda　⊕ **Coda**

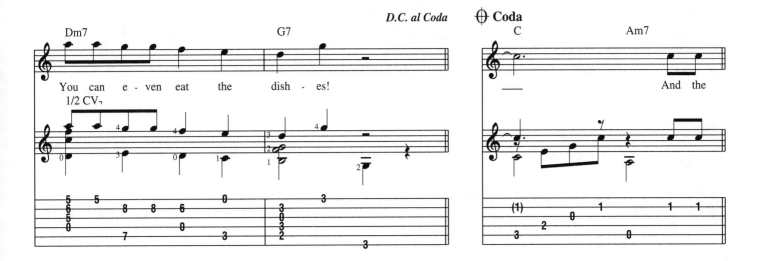

You can e - ven eat the dish - es!

And the

Outro

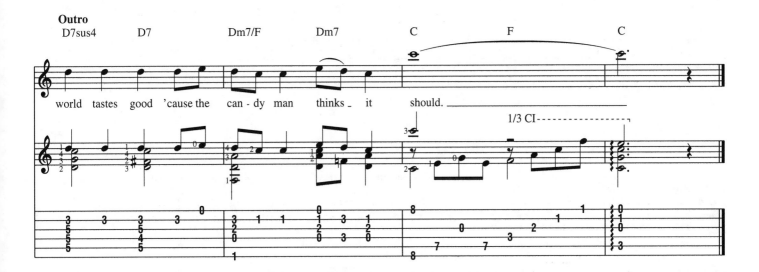

world tastes good 'cause the can - dy man thinks＿ it should. ＿＿＿＿＿＿

Additional Lyrics

2. Who can take a rainbow
   Wrap it in a sigh,
   Soak it in the sun and make a strawb'ry lemon pie?

3. Who can take tomorrow,
   Dip it in a dream,
   Separate the sorrow and collect up all the cream?

Casper the Friendly Ghost

from the Paramount Cartoon

Words by Mack David
Music by Jerry Livingston

1. Cas - per the friend - ly ghost, the friend - li - est ghost you know. Though
2., 3. *See additional lyrics*

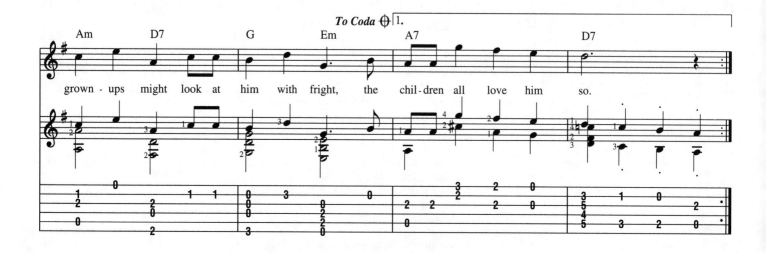

grown - ups might look at him with fright, the chil - dren all love him so.

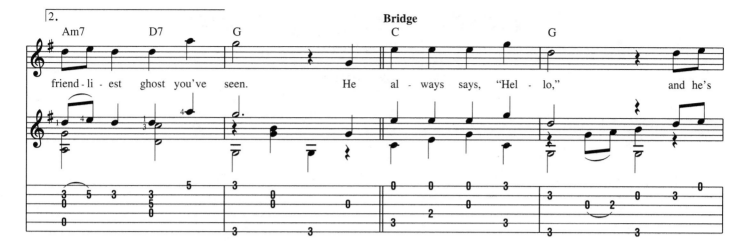

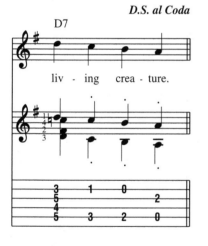

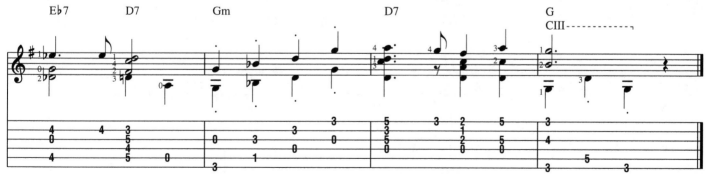

Additional Lyrics

2. Casper the friendly ghost,
He couldn't be bad or mean.
He'll romp and play, sing and dance all day,
The friendliest ghost you've seen.

3. Grownups don't understand
Why children love him the most.
But kids all know that he loves them so,
Casper the friendly ghost.

I Whistle a Happy Tune

from THE KIND AND I
Lyrics by Oscar Hammerstein II
Music by Richard Rodgers

⊕ Coda

I'm not a-fraid.

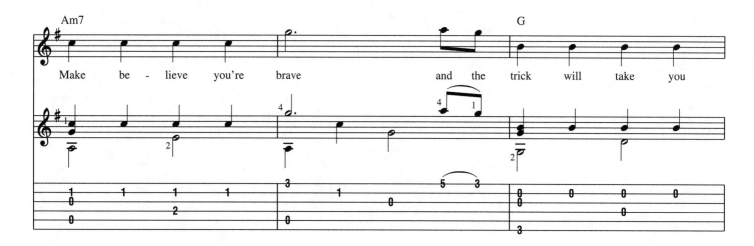

Make be-lieve you're brave and the trick will take you

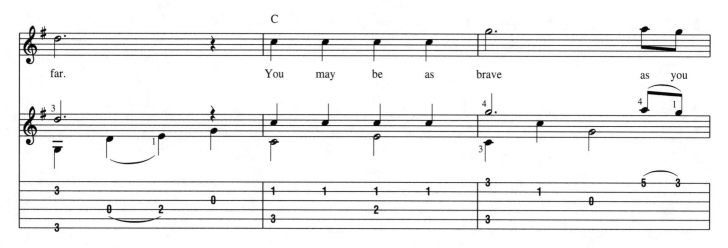

far. You may be as brave as you

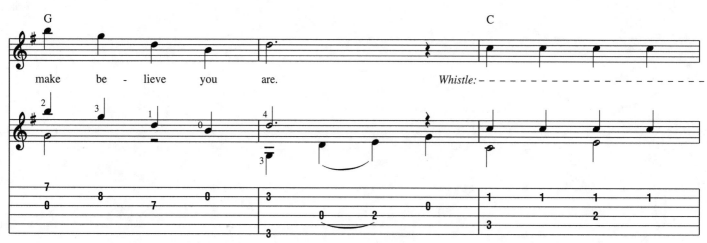

make be-lieve you are.

Whistle: - - - - - - - - - - - -

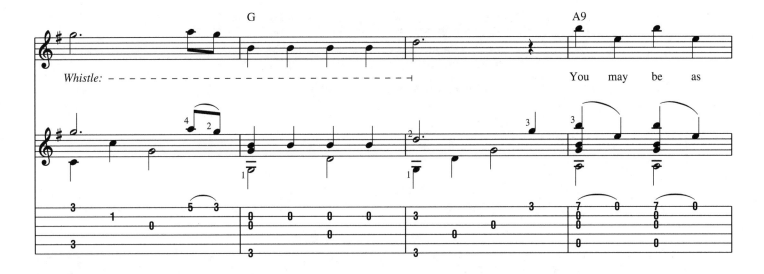

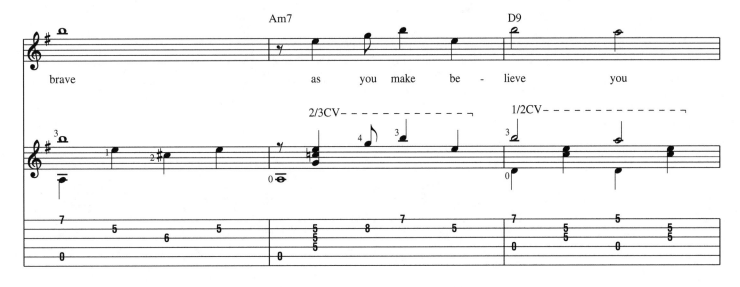

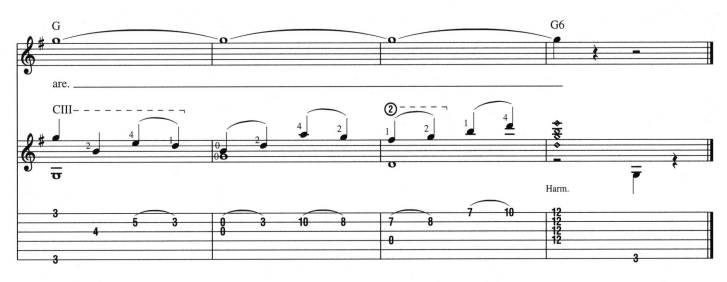

Additional Lyrics

2. While shivering in my shoes,
   I strike a careless pose,
   And whistle a happy tune,
   And no one ever knows I'm afraid.

3. I whistle a happy tune,
   And ev'ry single time,
   The happiness in the tune
   Convinces me that I'm not afraid.

I'm Popeye the Sailor Man

Theme from the Paramount Cartoon POPEYE THE SAILOR
Theme from the Paramount Picture POPEYE

Words and Music by Sammy Lerner

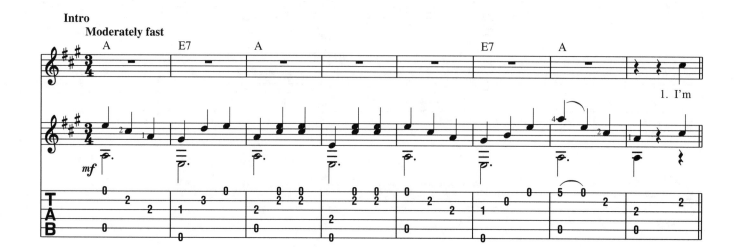

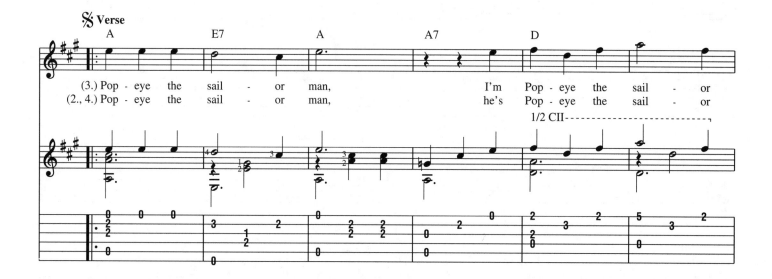

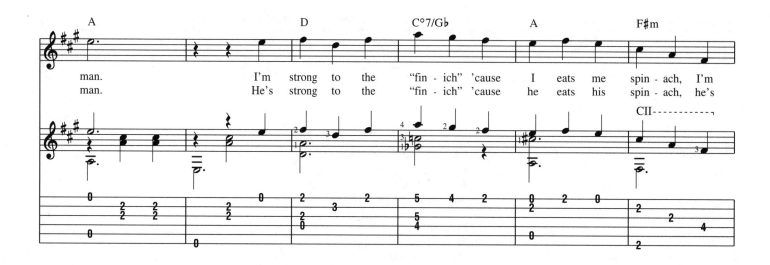

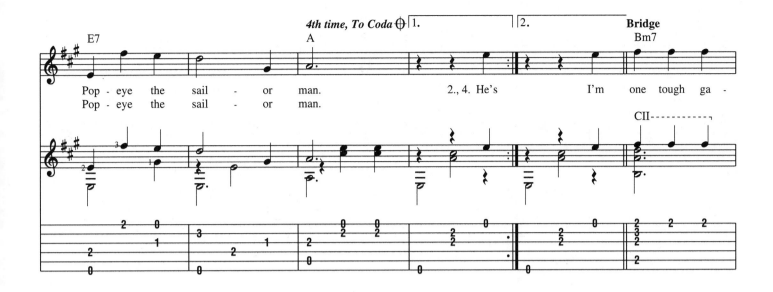

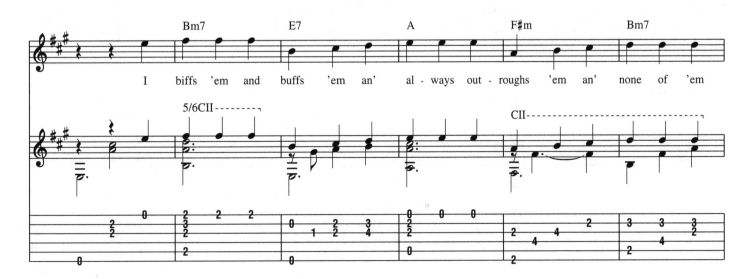

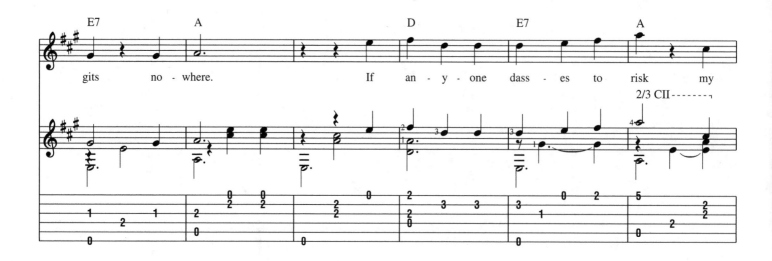

gits no - where. If an - y - one dass - es to risk my

2/3 CII- - - - - - -

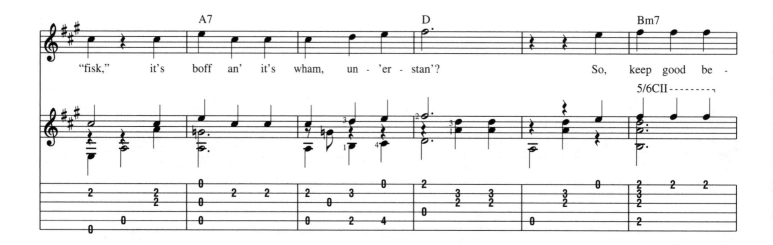

"fisk," it's boff an' it's wham, un - 'er - stan'? So, keep good be -

5/6CII- - - - - - - - -

D.S. al Coda
(take repeat)

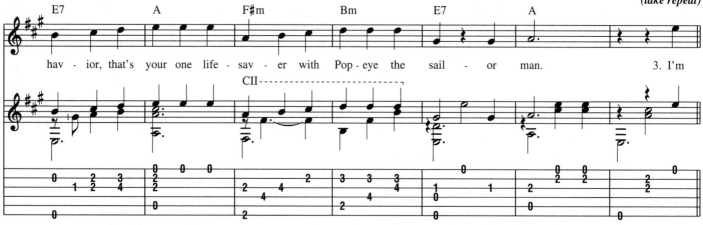

hav - ior, that's your one life - sav - er with Pop - eye the sail - or man. 3. I'm

CII- -

⊕ **Coda**

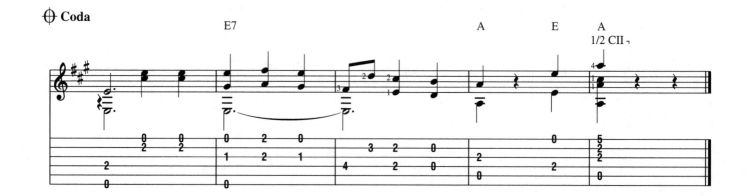

Mickey Mouse March

from Walt Disney's THE MICKEY MOUSE CLUB

Words and Music by Jimmie Dodd

It's a Small World

from Disneyland and Walt Disney World's IT'S A SMALL WORLD

Words and Music by Richard M. Sherman and Robert B. Sherman

world of laugh - ter, a world of tears. It's a world of hopes and a world of fears. There's so
just one moon and one gold - en sun, and a smile means friend - ship to ev - 'ry - one. Though the

much that we share that it's time we're a - ware. It's a small world af - ter all. _____
moun - tains di - vide and the o - ceans are wide, it's a small world af - ter all. _____

Chorus

Little April Shower

from Walt Disney's BAMBI

Words by Larry Morey
Music by Frank Churchill

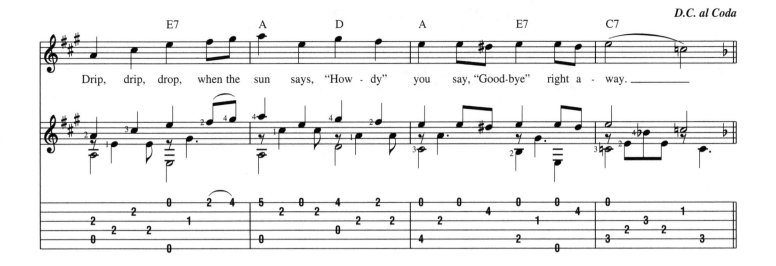

Drip, drip, drop, when the sun says, "How-dy" you say, "Good-bye" right a-way. _____

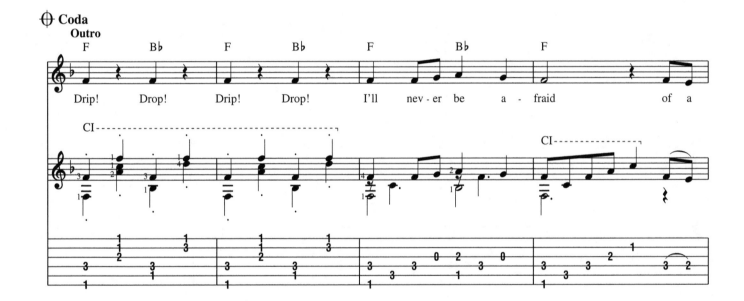

Drip! Drop! Drip! Drop! I'll nev-er be a-fraid of a

good lit-tle, gay lit-tle A-pril ser-e-nade. _____

My Favorite Things

from THE SOUND OF MUSIC

Lyrics by Oscar Hammerstein II
Music by Richard Rodgers

Verse

Slowly

1. Rain-drops on ros-es and whisk-ers on kit-tens, bright cop-per ket-tles and warm wool-en mit-tens; brown pa-per pack-ag-es tied up with strings: These are a few of my fa-vor-ite things.

when the bee stings, when I'm feel - ing sad, _____ I sim - ply re -

mem - ber my fa - vor - ite things and then I don't feel so

bad. _____

On Top of Spaghetti

Words and Music by Tom Glazer

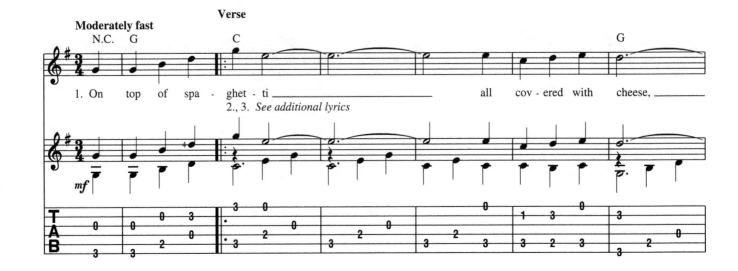

1. On top of spa-ghet-ti _____ all cov-ered with cheese, _____
2., 3. *See additional lyrics*

I lost my poor meat-ball _____ when

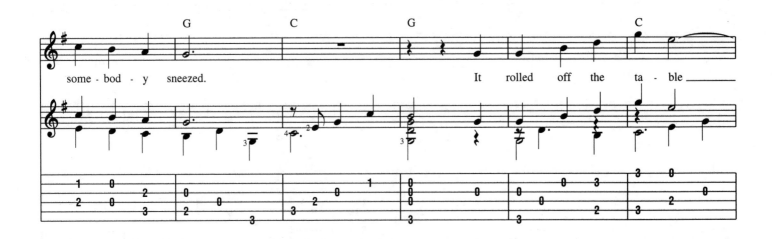

some-bod-y sneezed. It rolled off the ta-ble _____

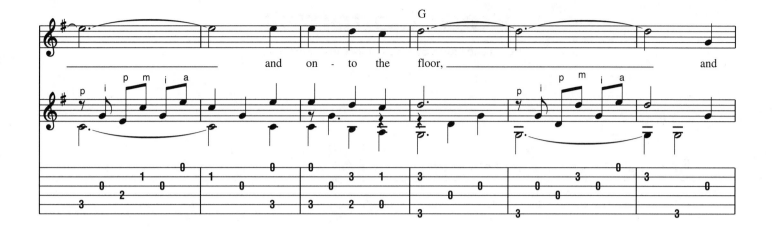

and on - to the floor, _____ and

then my poor meat - ball _____ rolled out of the door.

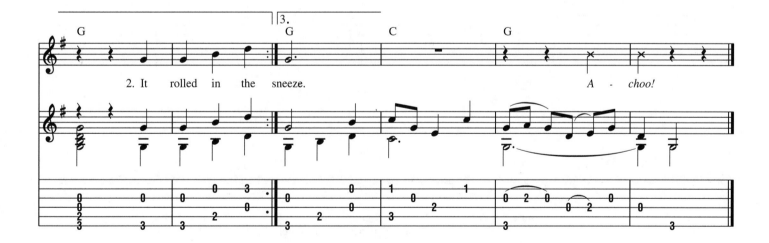

2. It rolled in the sneeze.   *A - choo!*

Additional Lyrics

2. It rolled in the garden and under a bush,
   And then my poor meatball was nothing but mush.
   The mush was as tasty as tasty could be,
   And early next summer, it grew into a tree.

3. The tree was all covered with beautiful moss;
   It grew lovely meatballs and tomato sauce.
   So if you eat spaghetti all covered with cheese,
   Hold onto your meatballs and don't ever sneeze.

Peter Cottontail

Words and Music by Steve Nelson and Jack Rollins

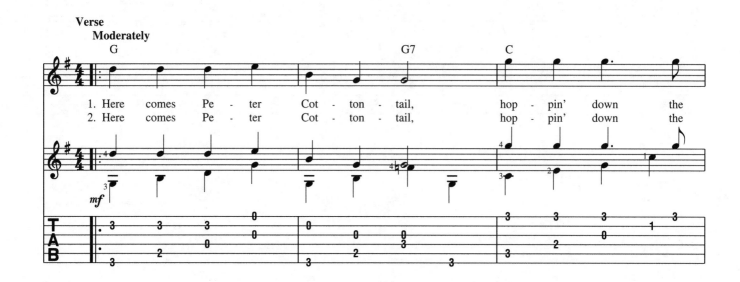

Verse
Moderately

1. Here comes Pe - ter Cot - ton - tail, hop - pin' down the
2. Here comes Pe - ter Cot - ton - tail, hop - pin' down the

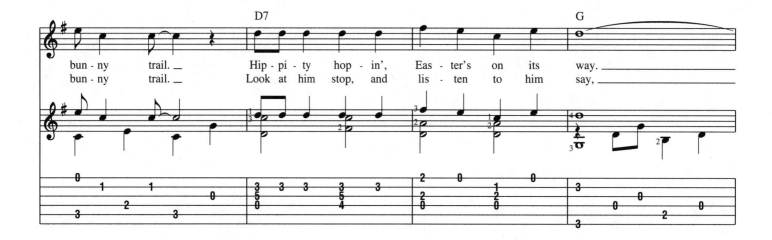

bun - ny trail. __ Hip - pi - ty hop - pin', Eas - ter's on its way. __
bun - ny trail. __ Look at him stop, and lis - ten to him say,

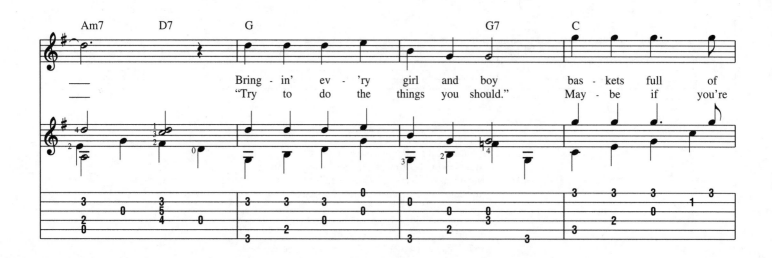

__ Bring - in' ev - 'ry girl and boy bas - kets full of
__ "Try to do the things you should." May - be if you're

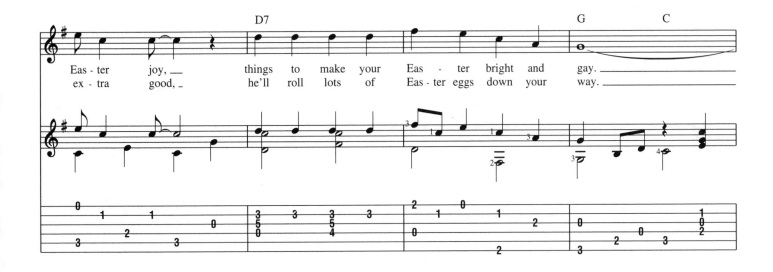

Eas - ter   joy, ___   things to make your   Eas - ter   bright and   gay. ___
ex - tra   good, ___   he'll roll lots of   Eas - ter   eggs down   your   way. ___

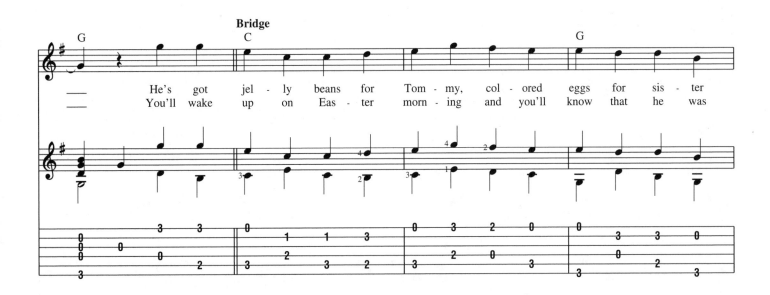

Bridge

He's   got   jel - ly   beans   for   Tom - my,   col - ored   eggs   for   sis - ter
You'll   wake   up   on   Eas - ter   morn - ing   and you'll   know   that   he   was

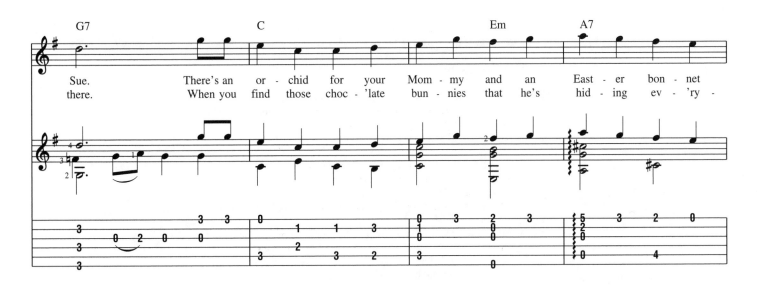

Sue.   There's an   or - chid   for your   Mom - my   and an   East - er   bon - net
there.   When you   find those   choc - 'late   bun - nies   that he's   hid - ing   ev - 'ry -

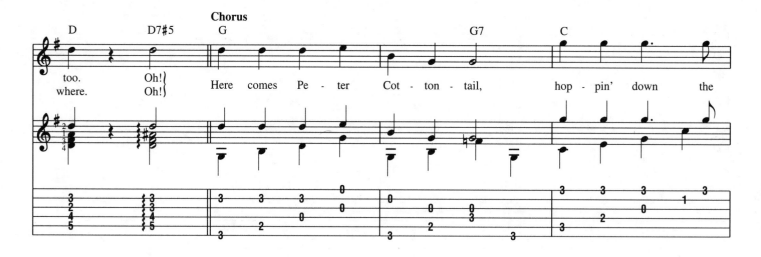

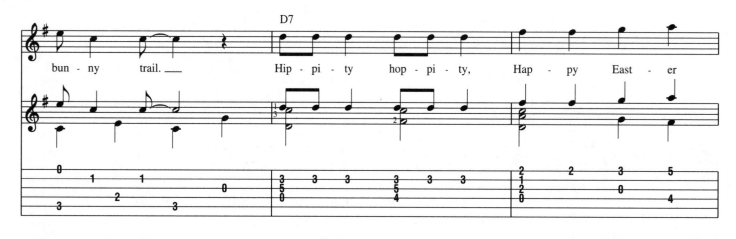

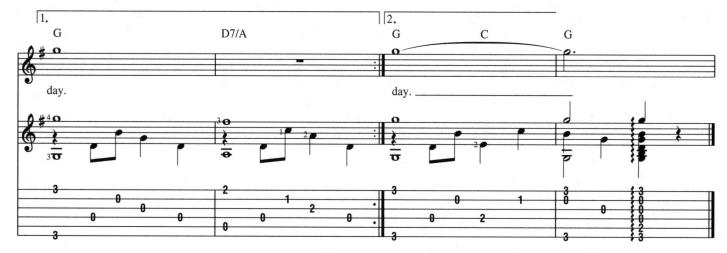

Year-Round Version

1. Look at Peter Cottontail, hoppin' down the bunny trail,
   A rabbit of distinction so they say.
   He's the king of Bunny Land, 'cause his eyes are shining and
   He can spot the wolf a mile away.

Bridge When the others go for cover and the big bad wolf appears,
He's the one watching over givin' signals with his ears.
And that's why folks in Rabbit Town feel so free when he's around,
Peter's helpin' someone everyday.

2. Little Peter Cottontail hoppin' down the bunny trail,
   Happened to stop for carrots on the way.
   Something told him it was wrong,
   Farmer Jones might come along and an awful price he'd have to pay.

Bridge But he knew his legs were faster so he nibbled three or four,
And he almost met disaster when he heard that shotgun roar.
Oh, that's how Peter Cottontail hoppin' down the bunny trail,
Lost his tail but still he got away.

Rubber Duckie

from the Television Series SESAME STREET

Words and Music by Jeff Moss

Intro
Moderately bright

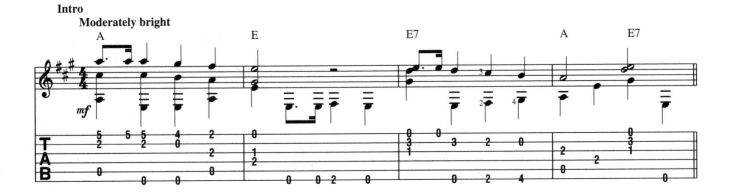

Verse

1., 2. Rub - ber Duck - ie, you're the one, you make bath - time lots of fun.

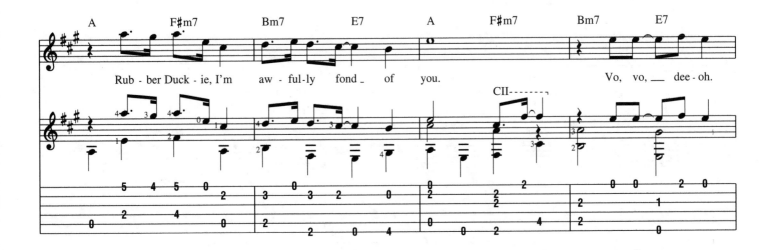

Rub - ber Duck - ie, I'm aw - ful - ly fond _ of you. Vo, vo, __ dee - oh.

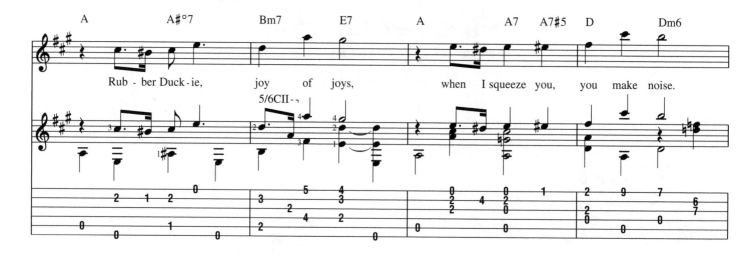

Bridge

Puff the Magic Dragon

Words and Music by Lenny Lipton and Peter Yarrow

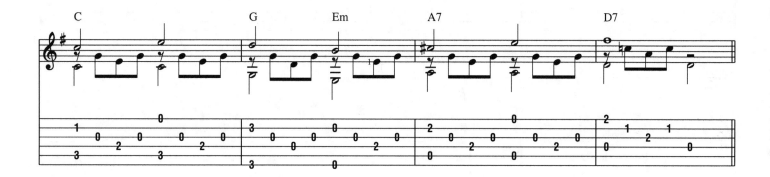

*3rd time, play verses 3. & 4. before proceeding to Chorus.

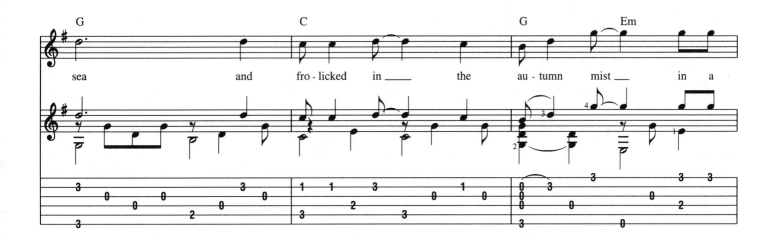

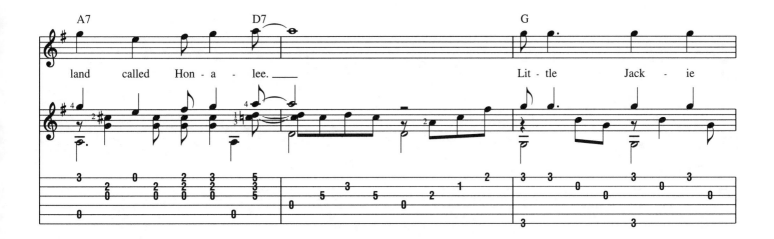

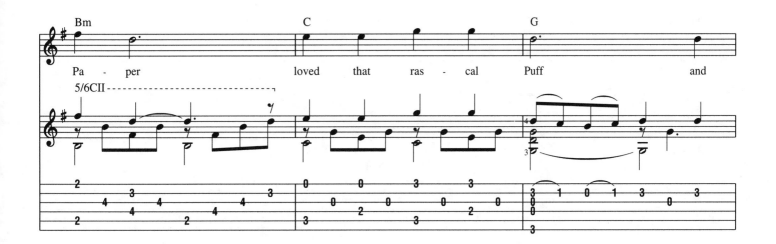

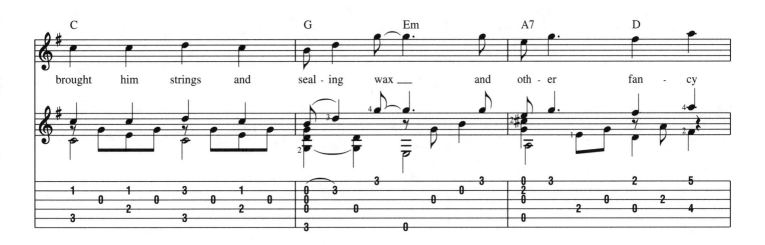

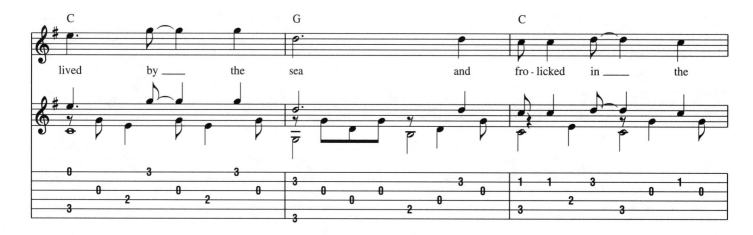

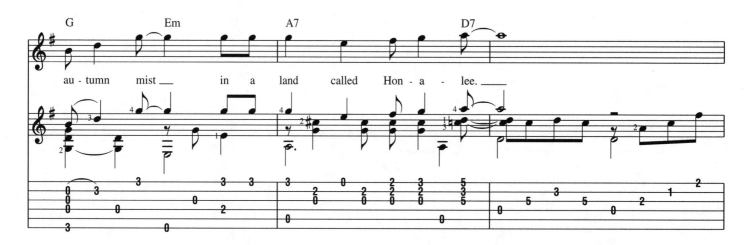

Additional Lyrics

2. Together they would travel on a boat with billowed sail.
   Jackie kept a lookout perched on Puff's gigantic tail.
   Noble kings and princes would bow when e'er they came.
   Pirate ships would low'r their flags when Puff roared out his name. Oh!

3. A dragon lives forever, but not so little boys.
   Painted wings and giant rings make way for other toys.
   One gray night it happened, Jackie Paper came no more,
   And Puff that mighty dragon, he ceased his fearless roar.

4. His head was bent in sorrow, green tears fell like rain.
   Puff no longer went to play along the Cherry Lane.
   Without his lifelong friend, Puff could not be brave,
   So Puff that mighty dragon sadly slipped into his cave. Oh!

The Return of Puff

5. Puff the Magic Dragon danced down the Cherry Lane.
   He came upon a little girl, Julie Maple was her name.
   She'd heard that Puff had gone away, but that can never be,
   So together they went sailing to the land called Honalee.

Sesame Street Theme

Words by Bruce Hart, Jon Stone and Joe Raposo
Music by Joe Raposo

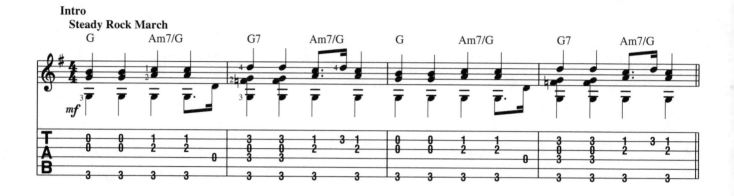

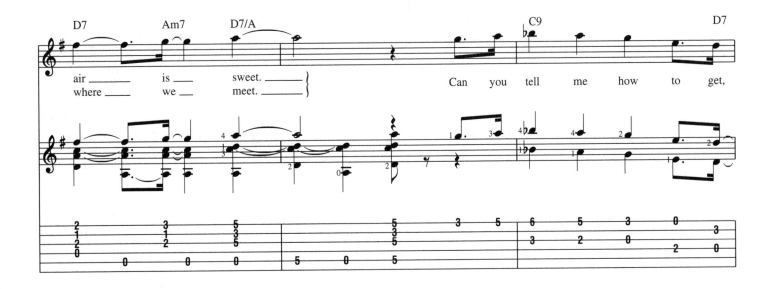

air ___ is ___ sweet. ___
where ___ we ___ meet. ___

Can you tell me how to get,

how to get to Ses - a - me Street? ___

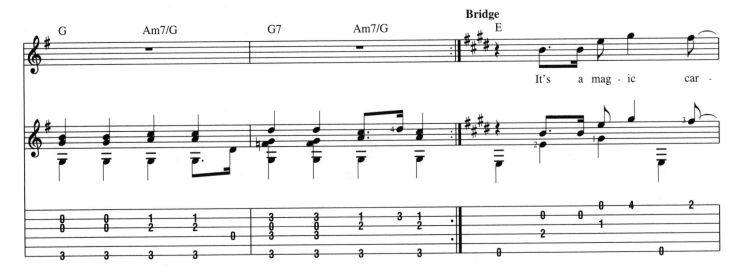

It's a mag - ic car -

D.S. al Coda

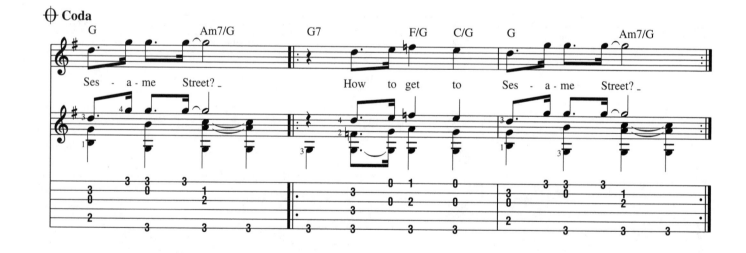

Ten Minutes Ago

from CINDERELLA

Lyrics by Oscar Hammerstein II
Music by Richard Rodgers

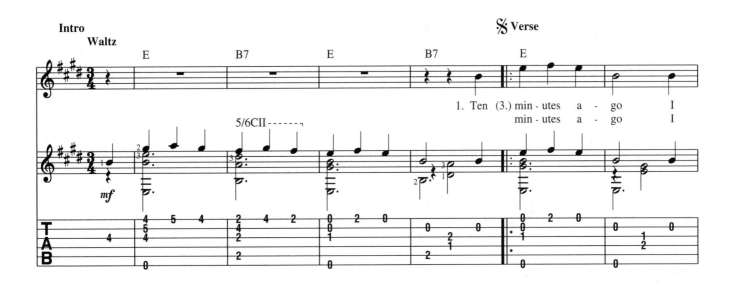

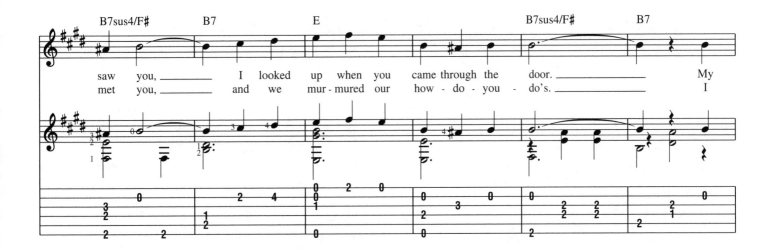

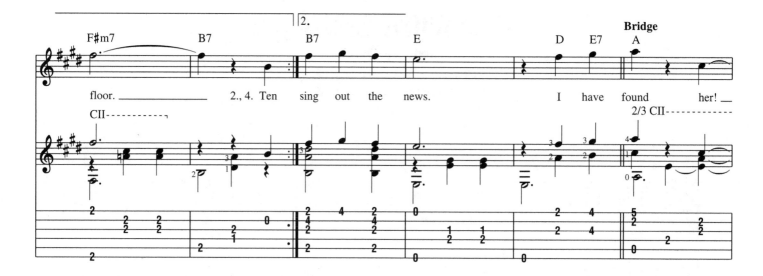

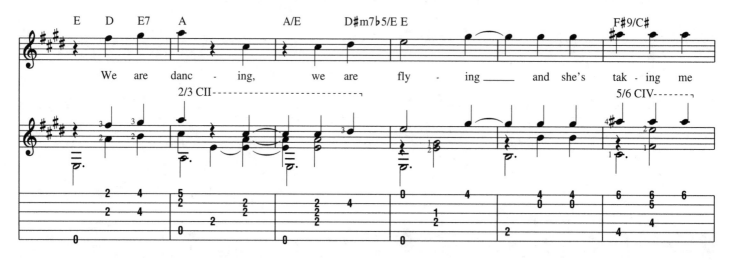

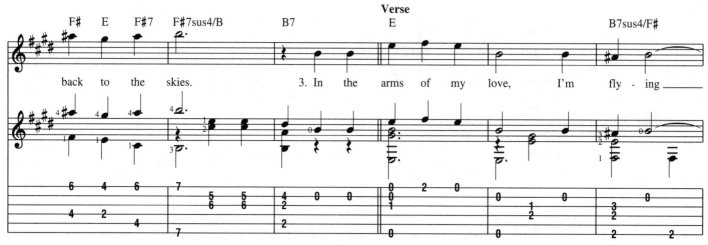

_over mountain and meadow and glen. _____ And I like it so

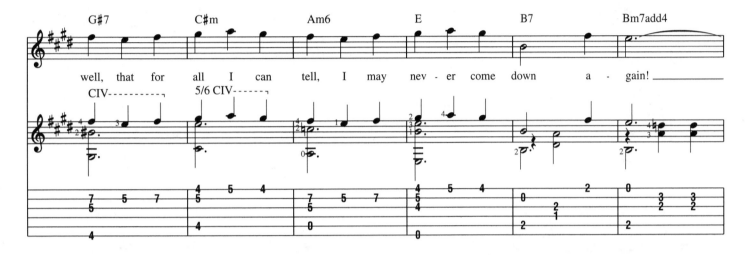

well, that for all I can tell, I may nev-er come down a-gain! _____

To Coda ⊕

_ I may nev-er come down to earth a- gain. _____

D.S. al Coda
(take repeat)

⊕ **Coda**

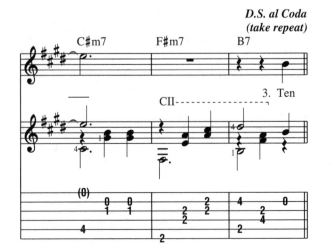

3. Ten

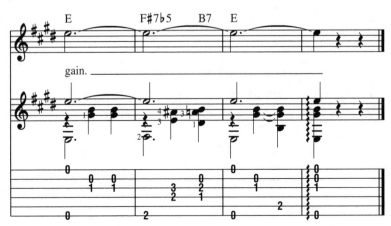

gain. _____

Under the Sea

from Walt Disney's THE LITTLE MERMAID
Lyrics by Howard Ashman
Music by Alan Menken

Just look _ at the world a-round you, right here _ on the o-cean floor.
But fish _ in the bowl is luck-y, they in _ for a wors-er fate.

Such won - der - ful
One day _ when the

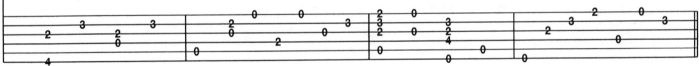

things sur - round you. What more _ is you look - in' for? }
boss get hun - gry, guess who _ gon' be on the plate? }

Un - der the

Chorus

sea, un - der the sea.

{ Dar - lin' it's
{ No - bod - y

sea.   Un - der the

sea.   Since _ life is sweet here, we _ got the beat here nat - u - ral -

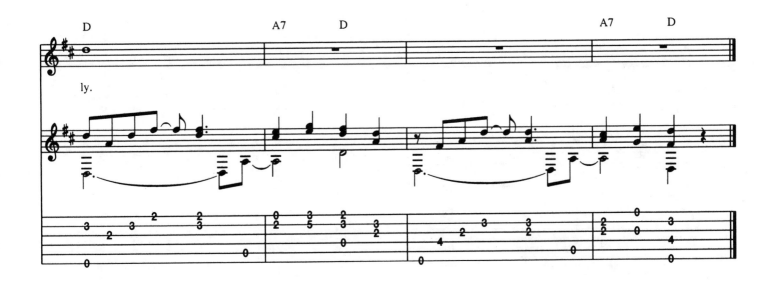

ly.

A Whole New World

from Walt Disney's ALADDIN

Music by Alan Menken
Lyrics by Tim Rice

Drop D tuning:
(low to high) D–A–D–G–B–E

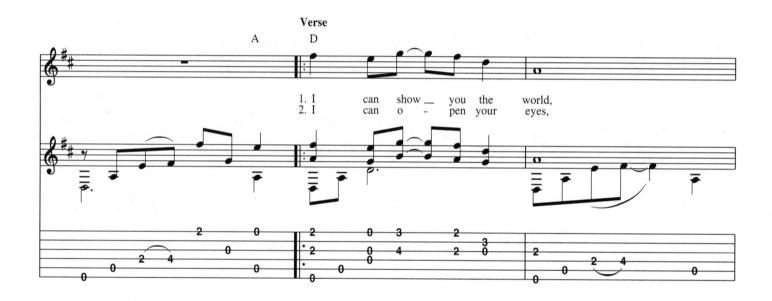

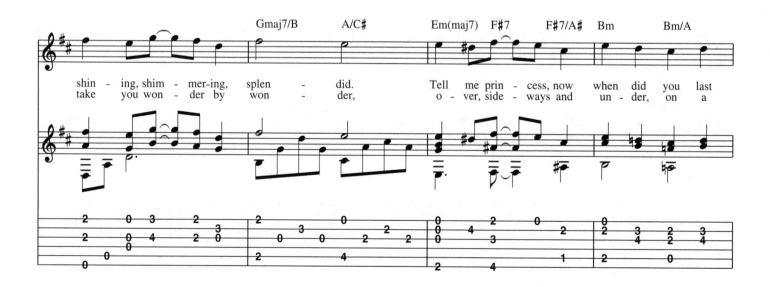

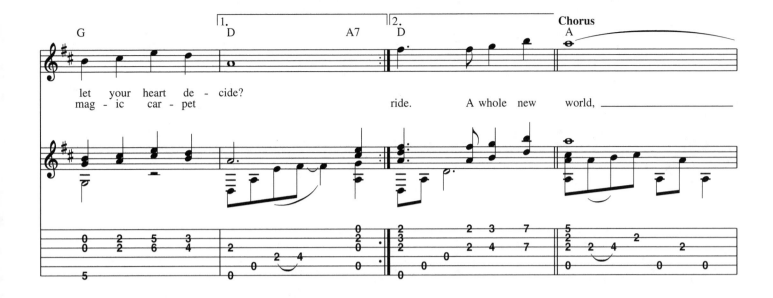

let your heart de - cide?
mag - ic car - pet ride. A whole new world, _____

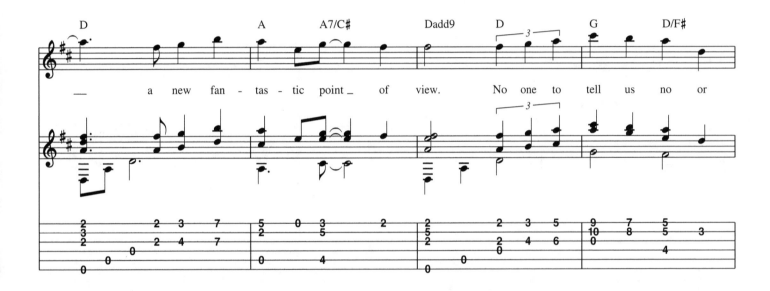

_____ a new fan - tas - tic point _ of view. No one to tell us no or

where to go, or say we're on - ly dream - ing. A whole new world, _____

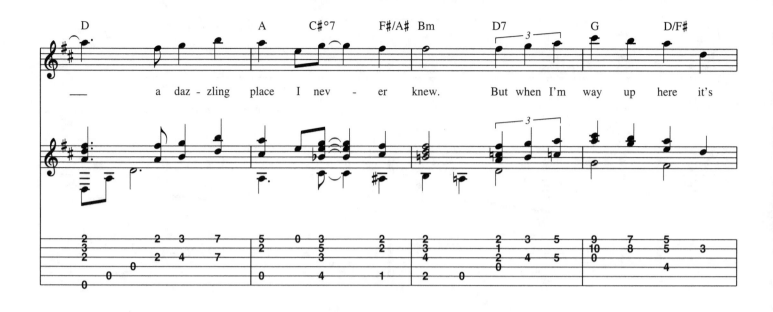

a daz - zling place I nev - er knew. But when I'm way up here it's

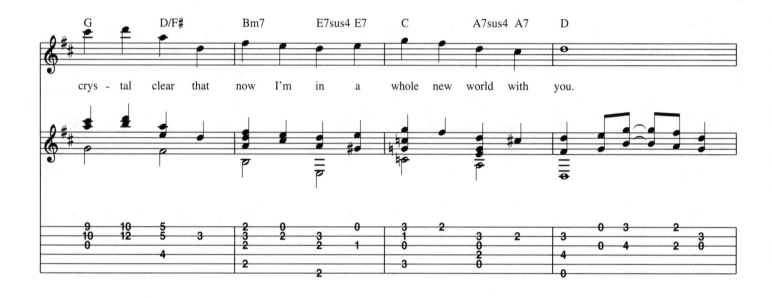

crys - tal clear that now I'm in a whole new world with you.

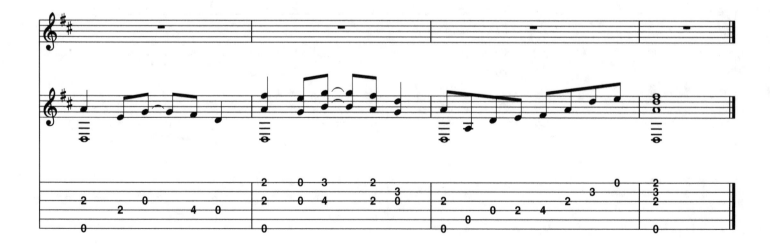

Yellow Submarine

from YELLOW SUBMARINE

Words and Music by John Lennon and Paul McCartney

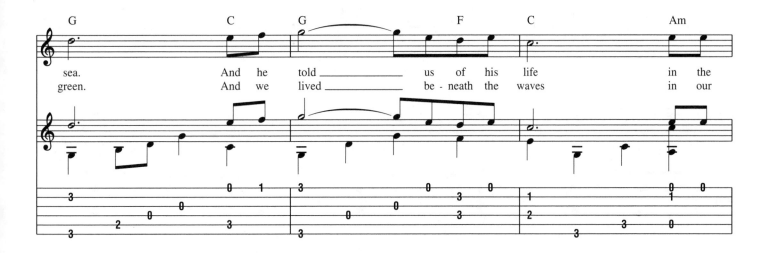

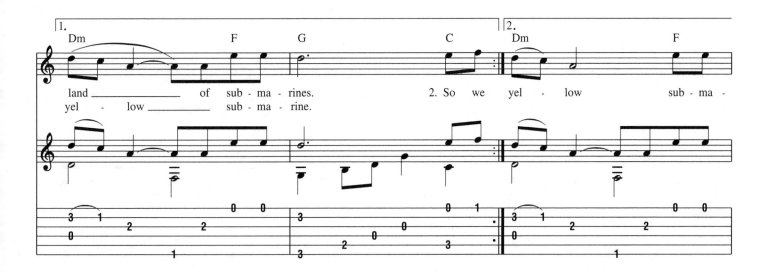

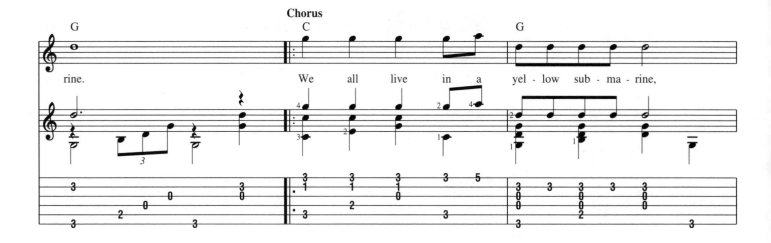

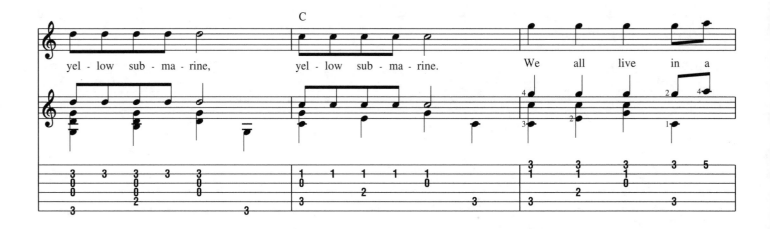

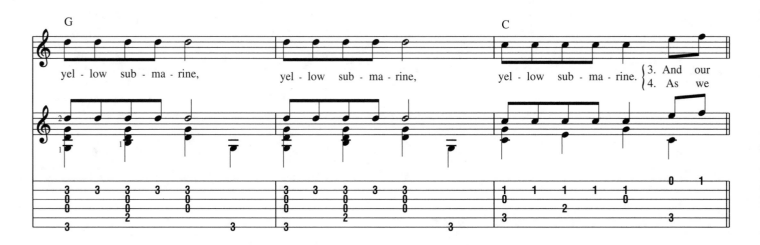

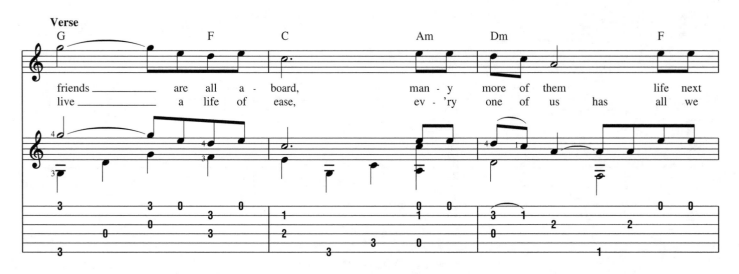

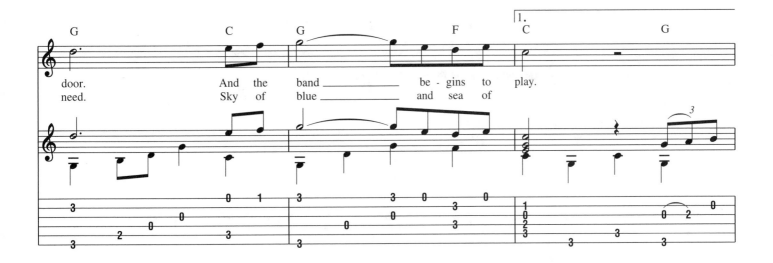

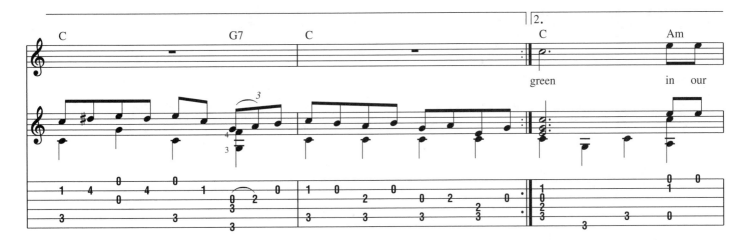

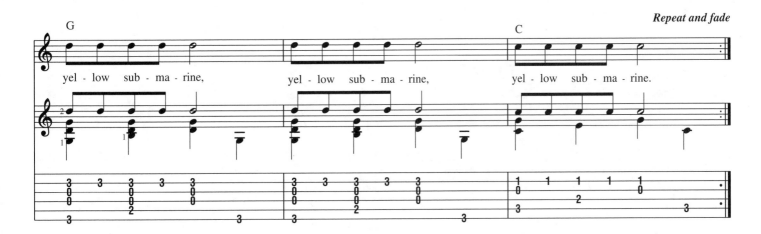

Winnie the Pooh

from Walt Disney's THE MANY ADVENTURES OF WINNIE THE POOH

Words and Music by Richard M. Sherman and Robert B. Sherman

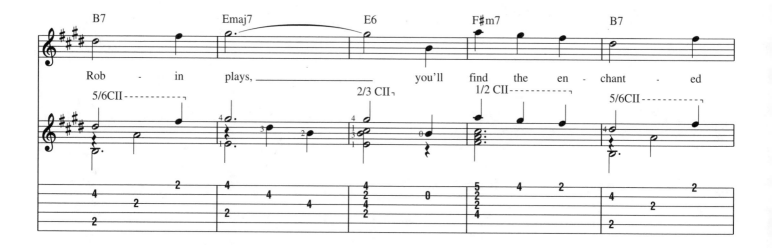

Zip-A-Dee-Doo-Dah

from Walt Disney's SONG OF THE SOUTH
from Disneyland Walt Disney Worlds' SPLASH MOUNTAIN

Words by Ray Gilbert
Music by Allie Wrubel

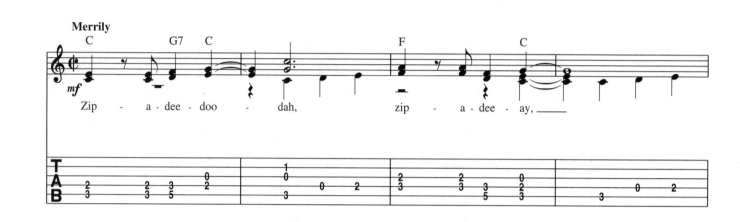

Zip - a - dee - doo - dah,   zip - a - dee - ay, ____

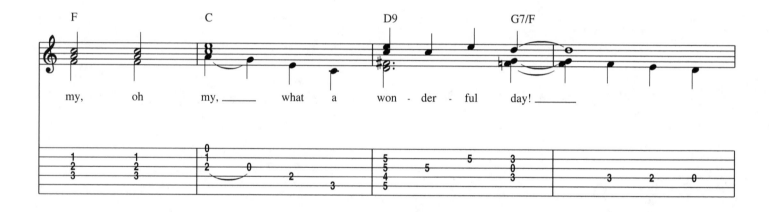

my,   oh   my, ____ what a won - der - ful day! ____

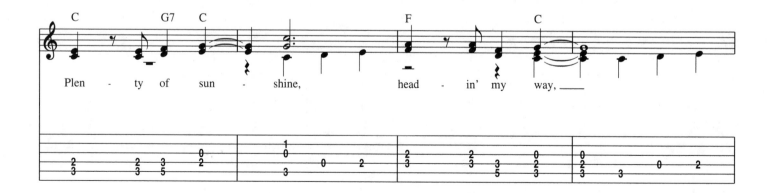

Plen - ty of sun - shine,   head - in' my way, ____

Zip - a - dee - doo - dah, zip - a - dee - ay! ___

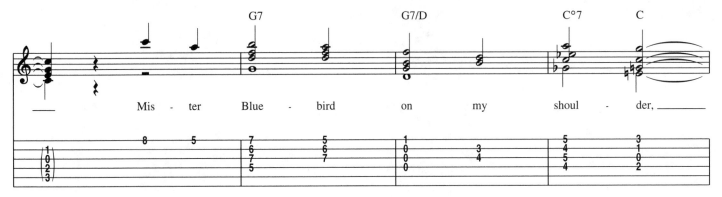

___ Mis - ter Blue - bird on my shoul - der, ___

___ it's the truth, it's "act - ch'll," ev - 'ry - thing is

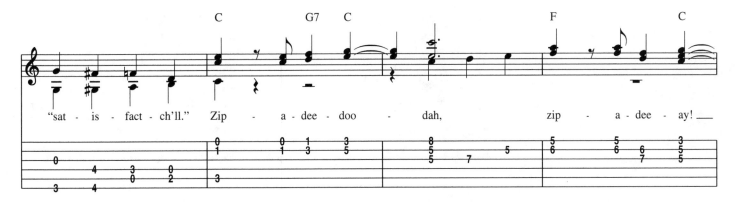

"sat - is - fact - ch'll." Zip - a - dee - doo - dah, zip - a - dee - ay! ___

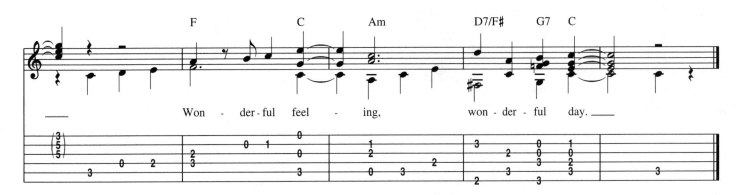

___ Won - der - ful feel - ing, won - der - ful day. ___

More Fingerstyle Favorites

from

HAL•LEONARD®

Acoustic Rock

19 contemporary acoustic hits in standard notation and tab: Angie • Best of My Love • Crazy Little Thing Called Love • Dust in the Wind • Fire and Rain • Landslide • Layla • Learning to Fly • Leaving on a Jet Plane • Maggie May • Norwegian Wood • Patience • Signs • Teach Your Children • Time in a Bottle • and more.

00699251..$12.95

American Folk Songs For Fingerstyle Guitar

25 songs, including: Amazing Grace • America The Beautiful • Home On The Range • I've Been Working On The Railroad • My Old Kentucky Home • When Johnny Comes Marching Home • and more.

00698981..$12.95

Best Latin Songs

17 great songs arranged for fingerstyle guitar: Bésame Mucho • Frenesí • The Girl from Ipanema • Granada • How Insensitive • Inolvidable • Malagueña • Perfidia • Summer Samba (So Nice) • Tico Tico • What a Diff'rence a Day Made • You Belong to My Heart • more.

00699132..$12.95

Broadway Ballads for Guitar

24 arrangements, including: All I Ask Of You • Bewitched • I Dreamed A Dream • Memory • My Funny Valentine • What I Did For Love • and more.

00698984..$10.95

Eric Clapton Fingerstyle Guitar Collection

12 Clapton classics for fingerstyle guitar. Includes: Bell Bottom Blues • Cocaine • Layla • Nobody Knows You When You're Down And Out • Strange Brew • Tears In Heaven • Wonderful Tonight • and 5 more favorites.

00699411..$10.95

Classic Blues for Voice and Fingerstyle Guitar

20 arrangements with guitar accompaniment and solos, including: Mercury Blues • Seventh Son • Little Red Rooster • Trouble In Mind • Nobody Knows You When You're Down And Out • and more.

00698992..$12.95

Contemporary Movie Songs For Solo Guitar

24 arrangements of silver screen gems, including: Endless Love • The John Dunbar Theme ("Dances With Wolves") • Theme From "Ordinary People" • Somewhere Out There • Unchained Melody • and more. Includes notes and tab.

00698982..$14.95

Country Classics

30 all-time country favorites: Always on My Mind • Blue Eyes Crying in the Rain • Born to Lose • Crazy • Folsom Prison Blues • I Walk the Line • If You've Got the Money (I've Got the Time) • King of the Road • Mama Tried • Rocky Top • Your Cheatin' Heart • and more.

00699246..$14.95

Disney Fingerstyle Guitar

14 fun favorites, including: Under The Sea • Beauty And The Beast • A Whole New World • Can You Feel The Love Tonight • and more.

00690009..$12.95

Favorite Hymns

29 inspirational favorites, including: Amazing Grace • Christ the Lord Is Risen Today • For the Beauty of the Earth • Holy, Holy, Holy • Let Us Break Bread Together • O for a Thousand Tongues to Sing • Were You There? • When I Survey the Wondrous Cross • more.

00699275..$10.95

Fingerpicking Beatles

20 favorites, including: And I Love Her • Eleanor Rigby • Here Comes The Sun • Here, There And Everywhere • Hey Jude • Michelle • Norwegian Wood • While My Guitar Gently Weeps • Yesterday • and more.

00699404..$14.95

Gospel Favorites For Fingerstyle Guitar

25 classics, including: Amazing Grace • Because He Lives • El Shaddai • How Great Thou Art • The Old Rugged Cross • Rock Of Ages • Will The Cradle Be Unbroken • Wings Of A Dove • and more. Includes notes and tab.

00698991..$12.95

Jazz Standards

20 songs, including: All the Things You Are • Autumn Leaves • Bluesette • Body and Soul • Fly Me to the Moon • The Girl from Ipanema • How Insensitive • I've Grown Accustomed to Her Face • My Funny Valentine • Satin Doll • Stompin' at the Savoy • and more.

00699029..$9.95

James Taylor

9 of his best, including: Carolina in My Mind • Country Road • Don't Let Me Be Lonely Tonight • Fire and Rain • Long Ago and Far Away • One Man Parade • Steamroller (Steamroller Blues) • Sweet Baby James • You Can Close Your Eyes.

00694824..$16.95

TV Tunes For Guitar

23 fingerstyle arrangements of America's most memorable TV themes, including: The Addams Family • The Brady Bunch • Coach • Frasier • Happy Days • Hill Street Blues • I Love Lucy • Mister Ed • Northern Exposure • The Odd Couple • St. Elsewhere • and more.

00698985..$12.95

FOR MORE INFORMATION, SEE YOUR LOCAL MUSIC DEALER, OR WRITE TO:

HAL•LEONARD® CORPORATION
7777 W. BLUEMOUND RD. P.O. BOX 13819 MILWAUKEE, WI 53213

www.halleonard.com

Prices, contents, and availability subject to change without notice. Some products may not be available outside the U.S.A.

0102

CLASSICAL GUITAR PUBLICATIONS FROM HAL LEONARD

THE BEATLES FOR CLASSICAL GUITAR

Includes 20 solos from big Beatles hits arranged for classical guitar, complete with left-hand and right-hand fingering. Songs include: All My Loving • And I Love Her • Can't Buy Me Love • Fool on the Hill • From a Window • Hey Jude • If I Fell • Let It Be • Michelle • Norwegian Wood • Obla Di • Ticket to Ride • Yesterday • and more. Features arrangements and an introduction by Joe Washington, as well as his helpful hints on classical technique and detailed notes on how to play each song. The book also covers parts and specifications of the classical guitar, tuning, and Joe's "Strata System" – an easy-reading system applied to chord diagrams.

_____00699237 Classical Guitar $16.95

MATTEO CARCASSI – 25 MELODIC AND PROGRESSIVE STUDIES, OP. 60 • _arr. Paul Henry_

One of Carcassi's (1792-1853) most famous collections of classical guitar music – indispensable for the modern guitarist's musical and technical development. Performed by Paul Henry. 49-minute audio accompaniment.

_____00696506 Book/CD Pack $17.95

CLASSICAL & FINGERSTYLE GUITAR TECHNIQUES

by David Oakes • Musicians Institute

This Master Class with MI instructor David Oakes is aimed at any electric or acoustic guitarist who wants a quick, thorough grounding in the essentials of classical and fingerstyle technique. Topics covered include: arpeggios and scales, free stroke and rest stroke, P-i scale technique, three-to-a-string patterns, natural and artificial harmonics, tremolo and rasgueado, and more. The book includes 12 intensive lessons for right and left hand in standard notation & tab, and the CD features 92 solo acoustic tracks.

_____00695171 Book/CD Pack $14.95

CLASSICAL GUITAR CHRISTMAS COLLECTION

Includes classical guitar arrangements in standard notation and tablature for more than two dozen beloved carols: Angels We Have Heard on High • Auld Lang Syne • Ave Maria • Away in a Manger • Canon in D • The First Noel • God Rest Ye Merry, Gentlemen • Hark! the Herald Angels Sing • I Saw Three Ships • Jesu, Joy of Man's Desiring • Joy to the World • O Christmas Tree • O Holy Night • Silent Night • What Child Is This? • and more.

_____00699493 Guitar Solo $9.95

CLASSICAL MASTERPIECES FOR GUITAR

27 works by Bach, Beethoven, Handel, Mendelssohn, Mozart and more transcribed with standard notation and tablature. Now anyone can enjoy classical material regardless of their guitar background. Also features stay-open binding.

_____00699312 ....$12.95

CLASSICAL THEMES

20 beloved classical themes arranged for easy guitar in large-size notes (with the note names in the note heads) and tablature. Includes: Air on the G String (Bach) • Ave Maria (Schubert) • Für Elise (Beethoven) • In the Hall of the Mountain King (Grieg) • Jesu, Joy of Man's Desiring (Bach) • Largo (Handel) • Ode to Joy (Beethoven) • Pomp and Circumstance (Elgar) • and more. Ideal for beginning or vision-impaired players.

_____00699272 E-Z Play Guitar $8.95

MASTERWORKS FOR CLASSICAL GUITAR

25 classical masterpieces for guitar: Allemande • Bourree • Canon in D • Jesu, Joy of Man's Desiring • Lagrima • Leyenda • Malaguena • Mazurka • Piano Sonata No. 14 in C# Minor ("Moonlight") Op. 27 No. 2 First Movement Theme • Ode to Joy • Prelude No. I (Well-Tempered Clavier)

_____00699503 ....$19.95

A MODERN APPROACH TO CLASSICAL GUITAR • _by Charles Duncan_

This multi-volume method was developed to allow students to study the art of classical guitar within a new, more contemporary framework. For private, class or self-instruction. Book One incorporates chord frames and symbols, as well as a recording to assist in tuning and to provide accompaniments for at-home practice. Book One also introduces beginning fingerboard technique and music theory. Book Two and Three build upon the techniques learned in Book One.

_____00695114 Book 1 – Book Only..$6.95
_____00695113 Book 1 – Book/CD Pack..$10.95
_____00695116 Book 2 – Book Only..$6.95
_____00695115 Book 2 – Book/CD Pack..$10.95
_____00699202 Book 3 – Book Only..$7.95
_____00695117 Book 3 – Book/CD Pack..$10.95
_____00695119 Composite Book/CD Pack...$24.95

ANDRES SEGOVIA – 20 STUDIES FOR GUITAR • _Sor/Segovia_

20 studies for the classical guitar written by Beethoven's contemporary, Fernando Sor, revised, edited and fingered by the great classical guitarist Andres Segovia. These essential repertoire pieces continue to be used by teachers and students to build solid classical technique. Features a 50-minute demonstration CD.

_____00695012 Book/CD Pack $17.95
_____00006363 Book Only..$6.95

THE FRANCISCO TÁRREGA COLLECTION

edited and performed by Paul Henry

Considered the father of modern classical guitar, Francisco Tárrega revolutionized guitar technique and composed a wealth of music that will be a cornerstone of classical guitar repertoire for centuries to come. This unique book/CD pack features 14 of his most outstanding pieces in standard notation and tab, edited and performed on CD by virtuoso Paul Henry. Includes: Adelita • Capricho Árabe • Estudio Brillante • Grand Jota • Lágrima • Malagueña • María • Recuerdos de la Alhambra • Tango • and more, plus bios of Tárrega and Henry.

_____00698993 Book/CD Pack $17.95

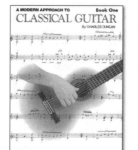

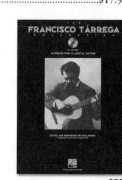

STRUM IT GUITAR

• AUTHENTIC CHORDS • ORIGINAL KEYS • COMPLETE SONGS •

The *Strum It* series lets players strum the chords and sing along with their favorite hits. Each song has been selected because it can be played with regular open chords, barre chords, or other moveable chord types. Guitarists can simply play the rhythm, or play and sing along through the entire song. All songs are shown in their original keys complete with chords, strum patterns, melody and lyrics. Wherever possible, the chord voicings from the recorded versions are notated.

Acoustic Classics

Play along with the recordings of 21 acoustic classics. Songs include: And I Love Her • Angie • Barely Breathing • Free Fallin' • Maggie May • Melissa • Mr. Jones • Only Wanna Be with You • Patience • Signs • Teach Your Children • Wonderful Tonight • Wonderwall • Yesterday • and more. 00699238 $10.95

The Beatles Favorites

Features 23 classic Beatles hits, including: Can't Buy Me Love • Eight Days a Week • Hey Jude • I Saw Her Standing There • Let It Be • Nowhere Man • She Loves You • Something • Yesterday • You've Got to Hide Your Love Away • and more. 00699249 $14.95

Celtic Guitar Songbook

Features 35 complete songs in their original keys, with authentic chords, strum patterns, melody and lyrics. Includes: Black Velvet Band • Cockles and Mussels (Molly Malone) • Danny Boy (Londonderry Air) • Finnegan's Wake • Galway Bay • I'm a Rover and Seldom Sober • The Irish Washerwoman • Kerry Dance • Killarney • McNamara's Band • My Wild Irish Rose • The Rose of Tralee • Sailor's Hornpipe • Whiskey in the Jar • Wild Rover • and more. 00699265 $9.95

Christmas Songs for Guitar

Over 40 Christmas favorites, including: The Christmas Song (Chestnuts Roasting on an Open Fire) • Feliz Navidad • Frosty the Snow Man • Grandma Got Run Over by a Reindeer • The Greatest Gift of All • I'll Be Home for Christmas • It's Beginning to Look Like Christmas • Rockin' Around the Christmas Tree • Silver Bells • and more. 00699247 $9.95

Christmas Songs with Three Chords

30 all-time favorites: Angels We Have Heard on High • Away in a Manger • Deck the Hall • Go, Tell It on the Mountain • Here We Come A-Wassailing • I Heard the Bells on Christmas Day • Jolly Old St. Nicholas • Silent Night • Up on the Housetop • and more. 00699487 $8.95

Country Strummin'

Features 24 songs: Achy Breaky Heart • Adalida • Ain't That Lonely Yet • Blue • The Beaches of Cheyenne • A Broken Wing • Gone Country • I Fall to Pieces • My Next Broken Heart • She and I • Unchained Melody • What a Crying Shame • and more. 00699119 $8.95

Jim Croce - Classic Hits

Authentic chords to 22 great songs from Jim Croce, including: Bad, Bad Leroy Brown • I'll Have to Say I Love You in a Song • Operator (That's Not the Way It Feels) • Time in a Bottle • and more. 00699269 $10.95

Disney Favorites

A great collection of 34 easy-to-play Disney favorites. Includes: Can You Feel the Love Tonight • Circle of Life • Cruella De Vil • Friend Like Me • It's a Small World • Some Day My Prince Will Come • Under the Sea • Whistle While You Work • Winnie the Pooh • Zero to Hero • and more. 00699171 $10.95

Disney Greats

Easy arrangements with guitar chord frames and strum patterns for 39 wonderful Disney classics including: Arabian Nights • The Aristocats • Beauty and the Beast • Colors of the Wind • Go the Distance • Hakuna Matata • Heigh-Ho • Kiss the Girl • A Pirate's Life • When You Wish Upon a Star • Zip-A-Dee-Doo-Dah • Theme from Zorro • and more. 00699172 $10.95

Best of The Doors

Strum along with more than 25 of your favorite hits from The Doors. Includes: Been Down So Long • Hello I Love You • Won't You Tell Me Your Name? • Light My Fire • Riders on the Storm • Touch Me • and more. 00699177 $10.95

Favorite Songs with 3 Chords

27 popular songs that are easy to play, including: All Shook Up • Blue Suede Shoes • Boot Scootin' Boogie • Evil Ways • Great Balls of Fire • Lay Down Sally • Semi-Charmed Life • Surfin' U.S.A. • Twist and Shout • Wooly Bully • and more. 00699112 $8.95

Favorite Songs with 4 Chords

22 tunes in this great collection, including: Beast of Burden • Don't Be Cruel • Get Back • Gloria • I Fought the Law • La Bamba • Last Kiss • Let Her Cry • Love Stinks • Peggy Sue • 3 AM • Wild Thing • and more. 00699270 $8.95

Irving Berlin's God Bless America

25 patriotic anthems: Amazing Grace • America, the Beautiful • Battle Hymn of the Republic • From a Distance • God Bless America • Imagine • The Lord's Prayer • The Star Spangled Banner • Stars and Stripes Forever • This Land Is Your Land • United We Stand • You're a Grand Old Flag • and more. 00699508 $9.95

Great '50s Rock

28 of early rock's biggest hits, including: At the Hop • Blueberry Hill • Bye Bye Love • Hound Dog • Rock Around the Clock • That'll Be the Day • and more. 00699187 $8.95

Great '60s Rock

Features the chords, strum patterns, melody and lyrics for 27 classic rock songs, all in their original keys. Includes: And I Love Her • Crying • Gloria • Good Lovin' • I Fought the Law • Mellow Yellow • Return to Sender • Runaway • Surfin' U.S.A. • The Twist • Twist and Shout • Under the Boardwalk • Wild Thing • and more. 00699188 $8.95

Great '70s Rock

Strum the chords to 21 classic '70s hits! Includes: Band on the Run • Burning Love • If • It's a Heartache • Lay Down Sally • Let It Be • Love Hurts • Maggie May • New Kid in Town • Ramblin' Man • Time for Me to Fly • Two Out of Three Ain't Bad • Wild World • and more. 00699262 $8.95

Great '80s Rock

23 arrangements that let you play along with your favorite recordings from the 1980s, such as: Back on the Chain Gang • Centerfold • Crazy Little Thing Called Love • Free Fallin' • Got My Mind Set on You • Kokomo • Should I Stay or Should I Go • Uptown Girl • Waiting for a Girl Like You • What I Like About You • and more. 00699263 $8.95

Best of Woody Guthrie

20 of the Guthrie's most popular songs, including: Do Re Mi • The Grand Coulee Dam • I Ain't Got No Home • Ramblin' Round • Roll On, Columbia • So Long It's Been Good to Know Yuh (Dusty Old Dust) • Talking Dust Bowl • This Land Is Your Land • Tom Joad • and more. 00699496 $12.95

The John Hiatt Collection

This collection includes 17 classics: Angel Eyes • Feels Like Rain • Have a Little Faith in Me • Memphis in the Meantime • Perfectly Good Guitar • A Real Fine Love • Riding with the King • Thing Called Love (Are You Ready for This Thing Called Love) • The Way We Make a Broken Heart • and more. 00699398 $12.95

Hymn Favorites

Includes: Amazing Grace • Battle Hymn of the Republic • Down by the Riverside • Holy, Holy, Holy • Just as I Am • Rock of Ages • This Is My Father's World • What a Friend We Have in Jesus • and more. 00699271 $9.95

Best of Sarah McLachlan

20 of Sarah's most popular hits for guitar, including: Adia • Angel • Building a Mystery • I Will Remember You • Ice Cream • Sweet Surrender • and more. 00699231 $10.95

A Merry Christmas Songbook

Easy arrangements for 51 holiday hits: Away in a Manger • Deck the Hall • Fum, Fum, Fum • The Holly and the Ivy • Jolly Old St. Nicholas • O Christmas Tree • Star of the East • The Twelve Days of Christmas • and more! 00699211 $8.95

Pop-Rock Guitar Favorites

31 songs, including: Angie • Brown Eyed Girl • Crazy Little Thing Called Love • Eight Days a Week • Fire and Rain • Free Bird • Gloria • Hey Jude • Let It Be • Maggie May • New Kid in Town • Surfin' U.S.A. • Wild Thing • Wonderful Tonight • and more. 00699088 $8.95

Best of George Strait

Strum the chords to 20 great Strait hits! Includes: Adalida • All My Ex's Live in Texas • The Best Day • Blue Clear Sky • Carried Away • The Chair • Does Fort Worth Ever Cross Your Mind • Lovebug • Right or Wrong • Write This Down • and more. 00699235 $10.95

Best of Hank Williams Jr.

24 of Hank's signature standards. Includes: Ain't Misbehavin' • All My Rowdy Friends Are Coming Over Tonight • Attitude Adjustment • Family Tradition • Honky Tonkin' • Texas Women • There's a Tear in My Beer • Whiskey Bent and Hell Bound • and more. 00699224 $10.95

Women of Rock

22 hits from today's top female artists. Includes: Bitch • Don't Speak • Galileo • Give Me One Reason • I Don't Want to Wait • Insensitive • Lovefool • Mother Mother • Stay • Torn • You Oughta Know • You Were Meant for Me • Zombie • and more. 00699183 $9.95

0102